Randi Glazer's 12 Strategies for Surviving a Career in the Business World

By

Randi Glazer

Table of Contents

What to Do When Co-Workers Create Conflict -- Intentionally or Otherwise	4
Be Respectful of Your Superiors, Even When They Don't Deserve It	7
On the Value of Being Perceptive	10
Know When to Trust Your Instincts	13
Picking Yourself Back Up	15
The Difference Between Leading and Managing	19
Be True to Yourself by Finding Your Own Niche	22
Understanding the Similarities Between Business and Marriage	25
Trust Can Be Both a Strength and a Weakness	28
Valuing the Knowledge and Expertise of Those Around You	31
The Benefits of a Lean, Efficient Organizational Structure	34
The Importance of Your Reputation	37

Dedication

To my father for helping shape my values and ethics to survive in the business world and to my mom who always supported my entrepreneurial spirit. I love you.

What to Do When Co-Workers Create Conflict -- Intentionally or Otherwise

Every profession is going to include people who are unsophisticated or simply uninformed to some degree, and the business world is certainly not an exception. Whether it is your colleagues, your superiors or other business professionals, you are likely to come into contact with someone who is uniquely capable of causing you to feel an acute sense of frustration during each and every interaction.

These individuals may make your job more difficult in any number of ways, but it is most often due to the drain on time and energy that comes from having to cover for their errors or to provide an explanation that corrects some misunderstanding. I have worked alongside many people who happened to possess this knack for disruption, and I have surely seen how different people react to a frustrating interaction.

I recall a quote I read again and again from one of my favorite business writers, Christopher Boggs.

"Crazy people don't know they are crazy. Stupid people don't know they are stupid. And crazy stupid people are really messed up (they are usually the "know-it-alls" in the office)."

Perhaps, some of your co-workers are not crazy and they are not stupid. Some of them, however, may lack certain pieces of information that lead them to make poor decisions or to adopt strategies destined for failure. The above quote merely illustrates that your co-workers likely have no idea their actions are misguided and may cause others to feel a sense of frustration.

I am reminded of a situation I once encountered when working with a referral person. I had become so frustrated with what I felt were inane and irrelevant questions that I started going over his head to get things approved. It became easier to do this than argue with him. This became problematic, because the only way I could do this without insulting him was to wait until he was out of the office and such an act was therefore completely acceptable on his part. Realizing that this was an impractical situation, I decided to adopt a patient approach in which I resolved to calmly sit down with him in order to thoroughly explain myself and ensure that he could clearly understand my line of thinking.

The strategy worked most of the time however, I almost lost my cool when he asked me a laundry list of irrelevant questions. Had this been one of my co-workers, they may have blown up at him and wound up insulting him for not understanding, but I instead took a few moments to explain the answers to all his questions.

Had I treated this person poorly and insulted his intelligence -- intentionally or unintentionally -- then perhaps he would not have been so willing to listen to what I was trying to explain to him. I invested more time during that single instance, but I saved a great deal of time for myself in the future by making sure he understood my values and ethics. We developed a stronger working relationship after this incident, and I found him to be far less frustrating to deal with from that point on. He did ask questions, but mostly for his own edification so he could continue to improve on the quality of his work.

While co-workers and internal customers can be difficult at times, learning how to interact with them in a positive and helpful manner can make an entire office run more smoothly. When you treat someone poorly, it can harm the entire work environment and make it a toxic place to work, so making an effort to be patient with even the most frustrating of co-workers is a critical strategy, particularly in the business world.

Be Respectful of Your Superiors, Even When They Don't Deserve It

If you are fortunate to work in any one place long enough, you will surely find that there is no such thing as a perfect co-worker or a perfect boss. The longer you stay in one place, the more likely it becomes that you will have a disagreement with a superior. This is merely a product of natural human interaction. While disagreements are a natural part of the human experience, there is a delicate way to go about this that will ensure you and your boss will be able to coexist in the future.

Even the best leaders are in the wrong from time to time, and it is often up to those working under these leaders to point out a potentially flawed strategy. If, however, I were to approach someone in a position of authority and tell them their strategy is imperfect without offering an explanation or alternative, then it is very unlikely anything positive will be accomplished by doing so. Someone in a position of leadership does not want to feel as though their staff is attempting to undermine them in any way, so a careful and thoughtful approach is most likely to be effective.

I have discovered the best way to assist a leader is to present options and alternatives along with a clear rationale that explains the benefit of such a strategy. Instead of saying, "this is better," it helps if you are able to ask, "Have you considered this option as well?" Presenting your idea in this way ensures your boss perceives you as offering an alternative idea rather than challenging their authority in some way.

Of course, there might be circumstances in which you could find yourself working for a leader who is completely closed off to the idea of suggestions from those "beneath" them. This is impractical for so many reasons, yet it remains likely that you will find yourself working for someone like this at some point in your career. If this is the case, then you will have to adopt a far more subtle approach in dealing with this sort of leader. There is also the distinct possibility you may need to consider moving on if your efforts and ideas are not appreciated in the way you feel they should be.

When dealing with a "closed-off" leader, you will need to take steps to present your ideas in a way that makes them feel as though it was their own idea to begin with. I once worked for an individual like this. There were several occasions when I went into their office and offered my own idea but framed it as though it was something they had suggested some time ago. I said something along the lines of, "Do you remember when you mentioned trying this approach a few months ago? Do you feel that might apply to this circumstance?"

I know it seems a little calculating to operate in this way, but it is the idea that is most important and presenting it in a way that will allow your boss to evaluate it on its merits. It just so happens that some bosses are unable to see the value in ideas presented by others, so the only way to get them to fairly evaluate all of the available options is to make them believe that ideas all come from the same place. You may not get credit for the idea, but at least you will be the beneficiary if the business improves as a result of utilizing the better alternative.

Some leaders can be incredibly difficult to work with or work for. If you decide to leave a company because of it, it may be tempting to tell them off just before you walk out for good and move on to something better. It may feel good in the moment, but burning bridges is never a good idea in the business world. You have no idea where you will end up years from now or where they will end up. You may very well cross paths with this person again, so always be as respectful as possible -- even when you feel it is undeserved.

On the Value of Being Perceptive

"When someone shows you who they truly are, you have to listen." – Oprah Winfrey

There are many times you may be surprised by just how cut-throat the business world can be, particularly if you fail to adopt a perceptive approach when conducting all of your professional interactions. This is why I have included the above quote from Oprah Winfrey because I have heard her voice repeating this phrase in my mind on many occasions in which someone gives the slightest hint of what they are really up to. In my personal life, I always look for the best in every person and believe that it is those qualities that make them who they truly are. In my professional life, however, I am less likely to waive away any red flags that come up during interactions. I believe you need to be hyper-vigilant in watching out for the qualities those around you may actively be trying to obscure.

I do not feel as though I am a pessimist in this way; instead, I feel I am more of a realist who realizes there will always be people in all industries that are willing to be dishonest, immoral and unethical if it means they are able to achieve the outcome they are seeking. Unfortunately, I have experienced this firsthand as well, and there have been many instances in which a co-worker, a superior or someone else has taken advantage of a professional trust with only their own benefit in mind. Once I learned to be perceptive to those brief glimpses that give away someone's true persona, I found it became much easier for me to avoid being taken advantage of in my professional dealings.

Does this mean that you should always be distrustful of others and believe there is always some ulterior motive guiding their actions? Of course not! Success in any profession requires some level of professional courtesy and cooperation. It is certainly not the case that everyone in your office is willing to destroy you in order to further their own career. It does mean, however, that you should be on the lookout for anything that may offer a clue into the motivations of those you work alongside.

Most people are honest and mean what they say, but there are always a small percentage of people who are willing to mislead others in order to get their way. All that is necessary for you to avoid being taken advantage of by these individuals is for you to be a bit more perceptive and to remember those instances in which someone revealed some aspect of their true nature. You can then use this information to guide your future interactions and to take precautions based on what they may have revealed about themselves.

It is in this way that you will be able to be more cautious

with those who make caution necessary and can continue to trust those who have genuinely earned your professional trust. There is a flip side to being perceptive since this will also make it quite evident that most people are interested in being helpful and cooperative and are not necessarily out to achieve their own selfish interest through unethical behavior or deceitful practices. It may seem overly simple, but your professional success may rely on your ability to recognize those worthy of your trust and those who should be approached with caution and trusted with only the greatest level of care.

Know When to Trust Your Instincts

I have been shown many times and come to believe that it is critical to simply go with your gut and avoid dismissing red flags in professional situations. After all, those red flags are absolutely there for a reason. Anytime something seems amiss or out of the ordinary, it is always best to take a few moments to step away and evaluate what may be wrong with the circumstance so that you can take the best possible course of action.

In business, it is particularly important for you to use your gut instincts. Trusting your gut can help protect a company from a poorly thought-out decisions made by others.

When I am asked to do something that goes against my values and ethics, my policy has always been to tell the person in a professional and direct way why I cannot do what they are asking.

Explaining your position in a simple logical manner makes it clear you take your position seriously and your aim is to do everything within your power to protect your company.

Some people have a hard time turning away business.

They only care about themselves, but even with that in mind, I have never had an issue after having articulated my concerns.

Learning how to trust your gut instincts is therefore of critical importance. If you ignore your gut and blindly trust the person presenting something without doing your own homework, you will be setting yourself up for failure. Never let another person do your job for you. We all learn and grow as time goes on. Make sure to give it a once over before moving forward. At the end of the day, you will be the one held accountable.

Picking Yourself Back Up

It is an undisputed truth that there will be times in which leaders have to make unpopular decisions in order to effectively lead. In many circumstances, these decisions will have an impact on you in some way, particularly if a leader is forced to cut down on personnel. If you survive the cutbacks, you will likely feel a great sense of relief at first, which is then quickly followed by the realization that those who remain are going to be expected to pick up the slack by handling the work that was once the responsibility of those who have now left the company.

Having enjoyed such a long career in the business world, I have heard every term imaginable for cutting staff: acquisitions, buyouts, mergers, downsizings and rightsizings, not to mention all of the other names that have been applied with the goal of somehow making you feel better about the fact that either you have been let go or that many of your co-workers have been let go. As a result, I have learned the importance of having the right attitude toward the unfortunate impermanence that is now prevalent in business and in the American economy, for that matter.

There was a time when a professional could expect to stay with the same company for 30 or 40 years before they retired. When I started in business, it was not unusual at all for many of my co-workers to never have worked at another company before working for the one they were at. Given the mergers and acquisitions that have plagued the business world, it is often not even economically feasible for this to be the case. My father, for example, worked as a Certified Public Accountant (CPA) his whole career and made partner at his firm spending 45 of his 50-year profession all with the same firm. Just one generation later and I can say I have worked for nine companies in total, only three of those companies are still thriving. Five of those companies no longer exist anymore having either been absorbed by another company or have gone out of business altogether and another company I worked for no longer does the same business, having pivoted its focus away from my area of expertise.

This change means that we have to live with the simple reality we are all "hired guns," and our business leaders will have to continue making cold decisions that are in the sole best interest of the company. These decisions will affect many lives both directly and indirectly, but, as Hyman Roth says in The Godfather, "This is the business we've chosen," so we must come to understand that change and impermanence will likely have an effect on us and our families at some point in time. In fact, once you have been affected by the cold decisions made by leadership, you will never forget that feeling that comes along with having to wonder how you will support your family and where you will find your next opportunity for employment. This is when you will find out who your friends truly are and may be happy to never have burned a bridge.

It was Friedrich Nietzsche who once wrote, "That which does not kill us makes us stronger." I believe my professional experience has made me stronger in many, many ways. It has made me more aware, more compassionate, more kindhearted and more sensitive to others who may be feeling the stress associated with any number of job-related concerns. It is not necessarily the most ideal circumstance to bond over, but it does form as sense of community and helps us realize that it is not always easy to separate our emotions from our professional lives.

As "hired guns," it also means that we have to be "ready on the draw" when business leaders in a company make an unpopular decision. When those decisions have an impact on you personally, it is important to remember that it is possible to pick yourself back up, dust yourself off and that eventually you will be better for having endured a difficult circumstance. With the benefit of my years of experience, I have come to realize that I can rely on my myself, my unique skill set and my professional approach to support my family rather than having to rely on the loyalty of a company that is very likely to be solely concerned with its profitability above all else.

The Difference Between Leading and Managing

It is not always the organizational structure that is responsible for inefficiency, and it is sometimes the case that you will encounter a manager who is motivated only by his or her own self-interest. Hopefully, it is not often that you will run into a manager like this, but if you do you have to be very careful. In the worst-case scenario, you may end up being scapegoated for something the manager failed to do or was incapable of doing, and in the best-case scenario the manager will take the credit for your hard work. While these are difficult circumstances and can create a highly toxic work environment, I believe that it is possible to reason with these types of managers in order to stimulate a positive change.

A few years back, I found myself working under a manager who fit this profile. After a few months of the entire office feeling an increasing sense of frustration, I requested a brief meeting with the goal of discussing her leadership style. I was very direct and let her know how my co-workers and I felt about the work environment, telling her that many of us felt as though our work was not properly valued or appreciated. I then explained that we all ultimately share the same goals and that our success will be viewed as the result of well-trained and dedicated employees working under an exceptional leader. This may not be the norm to confront a leader directly however, the situation became dire as staff started leaving putting more stress on the remaining employees.

After a long conversation, it became clear that she truly had no idea how she had been treating us, so she promised to change her leadership style as long as we promised to be willing to communicate with her on a more frequent basis. The result was a more efficient office that quickly became among the most productive in the company, which garnered the attention of upper management and ultimately earned her a promotion. Had we never said anything, we would have been forced to work under undesirable conditions with no hope for change, and she would have never understood the difference between leading a team and managing one.

This situation worked out, fortunately. However, there was no guarantee at the start our concerns would even be heard. It takes a strong person to recognize their weakness with the willingness to change and grow. It takes an even stronger person to speak with them about it directly.

Even though there are times in which it will seem that a manager is selfish and awful in just about every way, the truth is that they are likely to be rational people who are willing to make changes to their management style if it means a greater level of productivity from their employees. It is then up to the employees to communicate any issues they are having to their manager, otherwise nothing will ever change. In all likelihood, the manager probably doesn't even realize that a certain management style is alienating their employees and would happily make any necessary changes for the betterment of everyone involved. This requires, of course, a willingness on your part to speak up even when it seems incredibly difficult to do so.

Be True to Yourself by Finding Your Own Niche

I had the good fortune of doing business internationally. It was then when I first felt that I had found a professional niche in which I enjoyed the work I was doing and the opportunities it provided.

One of the greatest experiences of my professional career occurred when I experienced the benefits of extensive international travel. It took some time for me to reach that point in my career, and I feel that I was able to do so largely because of the manner in which I approached previous work opportunities and how I valued every opportunity to learn something new about the business world. This approach, combined with the professional philosophy I adopted very early on in my career, enabled me to get a great deal out of the time I spent in each position I have worked at in the business world.

As a professional working in international business, I traveled frequently and learned quite a bit about the way business was done overseas. Of course, I also got to meet and work alongside many interesting individuals as well, which I feel was an incredibly important part of my continued professional development. When it comes to feeling a sense of happiness that stems from your professional employment, there is nothing more essential than finding the right professional niche.

I have counseled many direct reports at review time asking them "what do you want to do next? What interests you? Where do you see your career going or where do you want it to go?" If the person is new to the business world, it is easier to counsel them because there is a world of possibilities open to them. If the person is older or has been in the business world over 10 years I usually tell them the following: *"Find your niche. Just because everyone else is doing the same thing doesn't mean it is right for you. Be where your competition isn't."* It's the same advice I give to growing a business. It's entrepreneurial to find your niche, to try different things and not get stuck in a position you are not happy with.

I am happy to report that following my own advice has been incredibly rewarding, and I feel that you will experience a similar benefit if you work diligently to find your own niche in the business world. This means that you will have to understand what is most important to you in a career and that you are also able to define what it is about a particular role that makes it rewarding on both a personal and professional level. It may be different for you, but for me I have always felt that there is a danger in accepting any position just because it was the more lucrative opportunity. I learned very early on in my career that money is more of a hygiene factor than anything else: you won't be any happier when you have it, but you will be unhappy when you don't.

With this in mind, I have always taken a job change based on the opportunity itself and not because it was the most lucrative offer. If the opportunity is one that will bring you joy, it will eventually bring you a financial reward as well. After all, it is always more likely for you to excel in a pursuit that brings you joy than one that doesn't, and an excellent work product typically leads to a financial reward. Along with a solid foundation and a culture that suits your professional needs, seeking out a company offering a position in a niche that brings you joy is the best strategy for creating a satisfying professional experience.

Understanding the Similarities Between Business and Marriage

You may remember how I mentioned the fact that my father worked for the same firm for 45 years before he finally retired, a span of time that in many cases exceeds that of a marriage. Even though a professional relationship lasting in excess of four decades has become increasingly rare, it is still important to approach your professional endeavors in the same way you would a marriage. A couple that is hastily married is much more likely to encounter challenges in the future than a couple that has taken the time to get to know each other and develop a deep understanding of their spouse, so getting to know and understand those you will be interacting with on a professional level can also make it more likely to achieve a similarly positive outcome.

While you may not have the luxury of a long courtship or a prolonged engagement, the same is essentially true in a professional setting. When you go into business with someone -- as an entrepreneur, an employee or in any other role -- you have to be sure that you have a thorough understanding of those you will be working for or with. Going into a business partnership is like getting married. The only way out is to dissolve the business. Knowing this will not prevent things from going wrong since there is no surefire way to predict future circumstances, but it will make it far less likely for it to be the case.

The question then becomes how to properly evaluate every opportunity to ensure that you pursue an endeavor that is most likely to go well. This can be difficult, particularly since you only have so much time to evaluate an opportunity before you have to make a decision. In these circumstances, I believe that you should do everything you can to get a sense of a company's values, structure and whether or not it is properly positioned for long-term success. This can be accomplished by developing a standard set of questions designed to yield the information you are seeking. If you are seeking employment with a company, you will want to know whether its financial foundation is strong and the opportunity is one that can lead to a long-term working relationship. If you are going into business with someone, you will want to engage in more than just the standard due diligence before agreeing to a partnership. Failing to do so can result in very serious consequences.

Of course, any relationship -- whether it is personal or professional -- requires a certain level of trust. This is true for all of the parties involved, but it will be up to you to develop a system for evaluating opportunities in a way that gives you the best chance to enjoy a long and lucrative professional career. Through the use of thorough evaluative measures along with a modest amount of professional trust, you give yourself the best opportunity for a successful career that also limits your exposure to the difficult circumstances inherent in any industry.

Trust Can Be Both a Strength and a Weakness

As I mentioned in the previous chapter, trust is something that is actually quite necessary in a professional setting. While this may be the case, you have to be careful regarding those you choose to trust and how much you choose to trust them. At the risk of sounding cynical, placing too much trust in others can lead to you being exploited by those in the workplace. In order to avoid this circumstance, you have to understand that there is a significant difference between being friendly with the people you work with and being an actual friend of someone you also happen to work with.

If you do not see someone or socialize with someone outside of work on a regular basis, then you shouldn't consider this individual to be a friend. Even though you may get along quite well during the workday, you should not share personal information with others unless you can legitimately call them a close friend. It is just too often the case that someone reveals something about themselves that quickly becomes fuel for the gossip mill due to the mistaken belief that the person they shared the information with is a close friend and not just someone they see at the office day after day. Keep your personal life personal, and only discuss professional matters while you are at work. Just a side note: it is also important to keep your work email and personal email separate, as well. Personally, I do not give out my work email to anyone unless I am doing official company business with them. If they are a personal contact, even if they worked at the company and left, do all your personal communications on your personal email.

Of course, investing the appropriate amount of trust in your co-workers can just as easily be a strength as well. The key is to ensure that your trust is placed in co-workers only as it relates to professional circumstances and not personal issues. It is perfectly acceptable to enlist the help of a co-worker on an account or to seek the advice of a superior on some work-related issue, but it is hardly a good idea to ask for the help of a co-worker regarding a matter that does not pertain to work or to seek the advice of someone in the office regarding some personal issue. It is unprofessional and places you at risk because of the tendency of gossip to spread quickly and the fact that office politics will play at least some role in the level of professional success you are able to achieve.

In some cases, your co-workers will attempt to draw you into the gossip mill against your will. It may start out with an inane question like, "So, what do you think of Lawrence?" How you respond to that simple question will surely get back to Lawrence and just about everybody else in the office, so it is helpful to have a neutral response always available at the ready. I have found the following responses are neutral enough that there is no possible way to get caught up in the inherent difficulties of office politics:

- "I find them interesting."
- "I enjoy everyone at work."
- "I don't know them well enough to comment."

Responses such as these will help you stay above the fray when it comes to the gossip that can sometimes disrupt the efficient operation of an office entirely. I have never been fond of the fact that offices operate this way, which may be part of the reason why I chose to work from home for so many years. The sad reality is that you are being evaluated on more than just your work product when you are part of an office; you are being evaluated on everything from meaningless social interactions to the frequency of your trips to the restroom. In an ideal world, you would be evaluated solely on the merit of your work, but the reality is that you have to be mindful of office politics and carefully manage your personal interactions within the office.

Valuing the Knowledge and Expertise of Those Around You

Being able to return the favor of the many mentors who guided me early on in my career is a large part of the reason I felt compelled to write this book and to share what I have learned over the years. I owe those who came before me a sincere debt of gratitude, and I simply cannot imagine having access to a more vital resource than the more experienced folks who were so willing to teach me and lend me a hand in so many different circumstances. I hope you will forgive my use of the following cliché, but I feel that this is just another way of "paying it forward" to the many professionals who are likely in need of mentoring.

When I entered the business world, I not only had the benefit of the countless mentors who had been around for many years, but also had the advantage of access to the thorough and frequent training programs offered by the companies I worked for at the time. Professionals who are new to the business world are very unlikely to have this sort of guidance available. My advice to you if you are just starting out or even if you just want to know more is learn as much as you can from the older, more experienced people around you; they have a great deal to offer and you will surely not be disappointed with the unique insights they are capable of providing.

Though it may be quite unfortunate, you must understand that much of your training will have to be self-directed if you are to be successful. This is a simple reality that you have to overcome, and the best way to accomplish this is to seek out the most experienced and knowledgeable professionals you work alongside with the hope of beginning a sort of informal mentorship.

Of course, this is easier said than done. It is now up to you, however, to find a mentor willing to take you under his or her wing, and this means that you have to understand how to approach a prospective mentor and how to request this type of help. After all, you will need to use a bit more tact and subtlety than just walking up to someone and asking, "Will you be my mentor? or "Would you be so kind to help train me."

Given the focus on efficiency, you have to remember to value your co-workers' time in the same way you value yours. After you have a sense of who is most likely to make a good mentor, drop by their desk or office for a very brief "pop-in" or approach them in a shared office space when you both have some downtime. Once you briefly explain that you have a few questions about your professional responsibilities or about business itself, you can then ask the individual if they are willing to meet before or after work for a work-related conversation over a cup of coffee (which you will offer to pay for, of course).

In nearly every circumstance, this initial conversation will spark an informal mentorship and will signal to others in your office that you are serious about your professional responsibilities. Without any further effort, you may find that other experienced professionals may drop by to see if you need anything or if you have any questions they can answer. This creates a valuable resource for you to use again and again, and there is also the added benefit of creating a greater sense of community within the workplace. This is something that everyone can appreciate, so feel confident in seeking out the vital assistance available through the most experienced professionals in your office.

The Benefits of a Lean, Efficient Organizational Structure

My experience in the business world has allowed me to see the benefits of a lean and efficient organizational structure in which leadership is in direct contact with employees and employees are endowed with vastly expanded opportunities to offer input into varied company operations. This leads to employees feeling that their contributions to the company are more likely to be properly recognized and appropriately valued. As I mentioned, my own experience with this type of organizational structure was few and far between, and most of my career involved working under multiple layers of middle management.

While this particular circumstance often led to a great deal of frustration, it also allowed me to develop a clear understanding of why every company should strive to adopt a leaner and more efficient organizational structure. Not only did I develop a more thorough understanding of this rationale, but I also learned how to properly adapt to a less efficient organizational structure in order to ensure that I remained an effective and valuable contributor in spite of the structural issues. When you focus on providing consistently outstanding work each and every day, there is very little that a poor organizational structure can do to adversely affect your professional reputation. It will be frustrating at times, but you should remember to focus on what you can control rather than what you cannot.

There are certain strategies that can be applied regardless of a company's chosen organizational structure, and I can tell you from experience that no one in a position of leadership likes to see their employees crowding by the elevator the moment the clock strikes 4 p.m. and signals the official end of the workday. This is not just a matter of keeping up appearances, however, as leaping from your desk at a set time each day means that you are either leaving work unfinished or that you finished up whatever you had been working on well in advance of the close of work hours.

Instead of attentively waiting for work to end, take the time to complete whatever you are working on before you depart for the day, and begin working on something new even when you find that the day's end is drawing near. This is a simple matter of professionalism, so keep this in mind the next time you see your colleagues racing for the elevator at the end of the day. It is also beneficial to employ positive motivational strategies on those around you with the goal of enhancing the quality of the work and the efficiency with which it can be accomplished.

This particular strategy leads to everyone feeling as though they are an important part of a team rather than an individual working amongst a larger group of individuals, which makes work more enjoyable and makes the office far more productive as a whole. When this is the case, there is no middle manager that will feel it necessary to exert his or her authority in a way that increases oversight and, often unintentionally, makes it harder to get anything done in a timely fashion.

While there are still many issues that have to be overcome in every work environment, it is my hope that the practical advice I have offered will make it easier to succeed in the business world. Every organization simply has to recognize the outstanding work of their employees, so if you adopt a single-minded focus on making consistently exceptional professional contributions, then you will surely reap a sincere and substantial reward.

The Importance of Your Reputation

When you move from one company to the next, all you have is your relationships and your reputation. The only legacy you have in business is what you leave in your wake. I have trained dozens of people over the course of my career. I have told every person how important their reputation and their relationships are. If you are a fair, consistent, honest, reliable and prompt person you will build a solid reputation. You will also build good relationships along the way, as well. Conversely if you do the opposite you will lose respect. To build a prominent image that is not what you want.

If you do what is right even if it may not be popular you will be OK. It is better to do what is right than do the wrong thing. Having good relationships does not mean doing the wrong thing. It means doing the right thing and sometimes delivering a tough decision in a kind way. You won't be able to do everything for everyone and that's OK. People will and do understand that on a human level. It is more important how you deliver the message. Your relationships and reputation depend on it.

I have built many relationships over the years and continue to build them. You cannot get around building relationships when you are doing business. As you move through your life building these relationships you will build a 'brand' of who you are and your reputation.

To be successful, you need to market yourself and your abilities to build your brand as a respected business person. Your reputation and your ability will help you to succeed. I have found that sometimes your relationships matter more. If you have strong ones they will take you through the tough times in business and through the business cycles.

Having a network of people you know is not the same thing as having a circle of friends. Your network will help you in business, but your friends will help you when you may be having a rough time. Be careful who you trust with personal information. It can affect your brand and your image.

I was told by a peer, "in life, you always meet twice". I believe what he said to be true because it has happened to me time and again. There will be people in life and in business who you may not want to see again, but you will. When that time comes and you do see them, do your best to be courteous, professional, and polite. If the other person says nothing to you or tries to ignore you, it's OK to go over and say hello and acknowledge the other person. No one likes to be ignored. You will be the bigger person by doing so and it will make it less awkward. You don't need to say anything more than "hello, nice to see you". After all, it's just business and even if it is not, you will still be doing the right thing.

Lastly, be true to yourself. Own your actions. Everyone makes mistakes. It is inevitable as you go through your career and through life. Admitting you made a mistake takes courage, but is necessary. Sometimes apologizing is the lubricant to a better relationship. I've learned that it's not what happens to you that makes you who you are, but how you react to it. My grandmother once said, "everyone is born with a suitcase of good things and bad things, but it how you carry that suitcase through life that matters." When you look back on your career and your life, be proud of how you carried your suitcase.

The views expressed herein are the author's own, and do not necessarily reflect the views of or relate to any specific organization.

www.ingramcontent.com/pod-product-compliance
Lightning Source LLC
Chambersburg PA
CBHW021447170526
45164CB00001B/423